The Story of
Truro Cathedral

G000162506

H Miles Brown
Ph.D, B.D., B.Sc.
Hon. Canon of Truro Cathedral

1991

with architectural contributions by
Lewis Braithwaite, M.A., M.I.C.E.

Tor Mark Press · Penryn

Other books in this series

First published 1991 by Tor Mark Press,
Islington Wharf, Penryn, Cornwall TR10 8AT
© 1991 Tor Mark Press
ISBN 0-85025-330-6

The text illustrations are reproduced by kind permission of the Royal Institution of Cornwall except that on page 12 which is reproduced by kind permission of the Cornwall County Record Office. The cover illustration is reproduced by permission of the Mary Evans Picture Library.

Printed in Great Britain by Swannack Brown & Co Ltd, Hull

1 'First catch your Bishop'

From whichever way you approach the city of Truro the Cathedral dominates the view. As you come by road from west or east, or up the river from Falmouth, or most dramatically as you come by train over the tall viaducts, the building rises impressively before you with its three towers and vast bulk in the very midst of the huddled houses, shops and commercial buildings.

Truro Cathedral stands as visible evidence of the renewal of the Anglican Church in the nineteenth century and is a living monument to the faith, patience and generosity of many Cornish people. It is also, as you can discover when you enter it, a centre of active Church life which extends its welcome far and wide. This book tells something of how it came to be so.

Of course, a cathedral is more than just a big church or famous building. It is a cathedral because of the *cathedra,* the throne or teaching chair of the bishop of the diocese, or the area marked out for his pastoral care. To be a cathedral, a church must have a bishop – the Apostolic representative, the link-man with the rest of the Church, the guardian of the Faith and the chief shepherd.

And a bishop of its own is what Cornwall did not have, from about 1050 to 1877! The story of how the county came once again to have a bishop is one of persistence in the face of government inertia, a story of frustrations and rivalries.

The Christian faith was probably first brought to Cornwall in the third or fourth century, when there is some evidence of Christian communities in the far west of the county and on the north coast. Early in the fifth century the Roman legions which had penetrated only tentatively west of Exeter were withdrawn. While the pagan Saxons and others slowly colonised England, pushing the Celts westward, in the far west the Celtic Church was extended and consolidated by travelling evangelists, hermits and teachers, male and female, who bound the Cornish, Welsh, Irish and Bretons into a community with a common faith and outlook.

Some of these Celtic 'saints' had been in episcopal orders, as abbot-bishops in the Celtic manner. About AD 840, Kenstec, Bishop-elect of the Cornish, made his submission to Ceolnoth, the Saxon Archbishop of Canterbury. After the Cornish had been subdued in the tenth century by Saxon conquest and infiltration, the normal diocesan pattern began to appear. The Cornishman Conan was installed at St Germans in 931, as Bishop for the Cornish, but after 1043 this bishopric was held jointly with that of Devon. Bishop Leofric moved the seat of the united sees from Crediton to Exeter in 1046; for the next eight centuries Cornwall became merely an archdeaconry in the diocese of Exeter.

The absence of efficient pastoral oversight, the weary journey of many miles with only rough tracks over bleak moors, the peculiar needs of the Celtic, Cornish-speaking, west, meant that to most of his flock the bishop was a distant and awesome stranger. This undoubtedly increased the decay in Church life which occurred in Cornwall, particularly after the shrines and collegiate churches were abolished under Henry VIII. By the mid-eighteenth century, the Church of England was in a parlous state, and nowhere more so than in Cornwall. John Wesley, whose Societies were intended to supplement, not supplant, worship at the parish churches, observed the needs of the Cornish and made 31 visits to Cornwall commencing in 1743, capturing the hearts and loyalty of many Cornish people.

In 1830, Exeter received a new bishop, Henry Phillpotts, who ruled with a firm but litigious style until 1869. One of his first acts was to undertake a visitation of his entire diocese in the summer of 1831, making enquiries and admonishing clergy and landowners to do their duty to the Church.

Phillpotts's energy and personality, coinciding with the Oxford Movement, brought the diocese into some shape. He instigated the building of 36 new parish churches to serve new centres of population, and it is from his time that we can discern the outlines of modern diocesan organisation, with its many activities such as choral unions, Church schools and parish guilds. Seeing the growing importance of Truro as a county centre, he built and enriched the Bishop Phillpotts Library, which still exists, serving clergy and laity. His remarkable force of personality gazes at us from his portrait, and his nickname *the Old Lion* testifies to it.

In 1840, Phillpotts proposed that the diocese of Exeter should be divided, having seen at first hand the crying need of the Church in Cornwall. The need for more bishops was apparent in the Church as a whole, and a Commission suggested that new bishops for Manchester and St Albans as well as Cornwall were urgently needed. Bishoprics can only be created by Act of Parliament, because the Church of England is the Established Church, and bishops become members of the House of Lords; when a Bill was introduced for the new Manchester bishopric, the Lords rejected it, thinking that more bishops in their number could affect the voting on contentious issues.

Meanwhile, John Wallis, vicar of Bodmin 1817-66, published statistics about the Exeter diocese. The population was estimated at 900,000. Wales, with only a slightly larger population, had four bishops. Cornwall, with 400,000 had none!

In July 1847, the Prime Minister, Lord John Russell, stated that it was intended 'if necessary' to nominate a 'Bishop of Bodmin'. Immediately the rival claims of Truro began to be aired. Truro had become a cultural centre, it was nearer the

The 1769 steeple and west front of St Mary's church before demolition. The cathedral nave now occupies the site of the churchyard and gates

populous mining districts, and it was on the main-line railway whilst Bodmin was on a branch line. Bodmin's parish church, admittedly noble, could not be enlarged, whereas St Mary's Truro could. Truro had other churches, so the cathedral would not affect parochial life. Truro's claims were supported heartily by the local clergy; but the Bodmin/Truro rivalry gave the government a good excuse for inaction.

The next step was a strange one indeed. In July 1854, Dr Samuel Edward Walker, the incumbent of St Columb Major near Newquay, who owned the advowson, offered his church, rectory and endowment for the new bishopric. It was one of the 'plum' livings in Cornwall, with a splendid church enriched in Tudor times by the Arundell family of Lanherne. At first the offer was greeted with enthusiasm: a rally of the clergy was held in Truro, which prompted Edward Carlyon, a prominent lawyer of St Austell, to ask why the laity should not also be called together. Carlyon remained a tireless worker for the diocese and cathedral for the next fifty years.

Bishop Phillpotts gave his support to the idea of using St Columb, and was ready to forego £500 of his income. (Cynics have suggested he stood to save at least that in travelling expenses!) Finally, in March 1855 the recommendation of the Archbishop's Commission was presented to the Government. And there it rested.

In 1859 the matter was again pressed in public, at a meeting in Bodmin. A booklet written by Prebendary Arthur Tatham outlining the case for a bishopric was adopted as a summary of the views of the large gathering. A deputation, led by the Earl of St Germans, visited the Prime Minister Lord Palmerston. He kept them waiting, then came down unshaved, almost unwashed, and his answer sent them away in despair: 'Gentlemen, you must do what Mrs Glasse said, first catch your hare – first catch your bishop.' Clearly he had not only misunderstood their request, but was totally unsympathetic to their purpose.

But it began to appear doubtful whether Dr Walker's offer could ever materialise. He had inherited a fortune from his father and invested much of it in unsuccessful property speculation; in 1855 he found it necessary to retire to the Continent and his St Columb living was temporarily sequestrated. On the Ladbroke estate in west London he had begun building a church, which stood amid unmade roads and roofless houses and was nicknamed All Sinners in the Mud.

The proposal to use St Columb foundered, and perhaps it was as well, since its only real virtue had been its neutrality in the Bodmin/Truro dispute.

In 1863 the Archbishop came himself to see Cornwall's need, but despite every appeal the government would not move. The succeeding years of indifference to their pleas were hard for the Cornish to bear, especially as opposition in high quarters seemed to be increasing rather than decreasing.

Bishop Phillpotts died in 1869. Why should his successor, Frederick Temple, be weighed down by responsibility for the largest diocese in extent of any in the country? Agitation began again, with renewed vigour. In 1875 Edmund Carlyon called a meeting in Plymouth to forward the scheme for division, and as a result a new deputation called on Disraeli, now Prime Minister. They were received more favourably than their predecessors, and it was made clear that the only hesitation arose from the need to establish an endowment for the new See, since nothing would be available from government funds.

In 1876 it was announced that Lady Rolle of Exmouth, herself a Cornishwoman, had given a large sum, reputedly £40,000, towards the endowment, and Bishop Temple wrote to every incumbent in the Diocese of Exeter asking for further funds. There was an immediate response. At last, in August 1876, a Bill was enacted establishing the Diocese of Truro.

The long years of frustrated effort and the faithful work of so many devoted supporters had at last been rewarded. The old church of St Mary in Truro was constituted as the Cathedral of the diocese.

But who was to be the first Bishop of Truro? As usual many names were mentioned by gossips and journalists, but it was no surprise when Edward White Benson was chosen.

2 The Bishop and the Architect

On his first day in Cornwall, 21 December 1876, Benson tactfully called on the rector of St Mary's, Clement Fox Harvey, in the Georgian rectory since demolished to make way for the cathedral nave. He also introduced himself to some of the leading citizens. Many were delighted that a new era was opening and that the Church of England was reawakening with fresh zeal, but some nonconformists feared that their

7

Bishop Edward White Benson

ascendency in the county might be challenged. It was not an age of comfortable ecumenism.

Benson lodged at Kenwyn Vicarage, now Copeland Court, that gracious house with a grand view of the town below which John Wesley, entertained there, had described as 'fit for a nobleman'. Richard Vautier, the vicar, later gave up this house for the residence of the new bishop who, in sensitivity to the Celtic background, renamed it in (poor) Cornish *Lis Escop,* Bishop's Court.

THE STORY OF TRURO CATHEDRAL

Benson was born near Birmingham in 1829, the son of a scientific chemist. From King Edward's School, Birmingham, he went to Cambridge as an undergraduate, and there faced sudden destitution. His father died bankrupt, and his mother and sister soon after. Benson was left responsible for the remaining five members of the family. Happily some well-to-do cousins came to the rescue. After a brilliant career at Cambridge, Benson went as assistant master to Rugby under Dr Goulburn. He had taken Holy Orders, being made deacon in 1853 and priest in 1857. As a result of his work at Rugby he was recommended as first Head of Wellington College, founded as a memorial to the Duke of Wellington as a school for the sons of officers. The Prince Consort was interested in the College project, and at his suggestion Benson spent a year in Germany studying educational methods there. He began work at Wellington in 1859 and was married the same year.

Under Benson, the College flourished. His creative powers, strength of character and sensitivity found scope in the development of the new school, which he ruled with a rod of iron. It was soon in the front rank of English schools.

In 1873 Benson resigned from the College on being appointed Chancellor and Residentiary Canon at Lincoln Cathedral under Bishop Wordsworth. It was intended that he would start a new theological college for the training of priests. The ancient cathedral, its statutes dating from medieval times, its customs and associates, clerical and lay, were to him of absorbing interest. He developed a romantic love of cathedrals and rejoiced that in his time they were awakening from centres of scholarly slumber to become vital parts of the renewing church. He found in his work necessary contacts with all ranks and classes in the city and developed a pastoral care which his previous work had not made a necessity. His Sunday afternoon sermons, simple and earnest, attracted large crowds of artisans and townsfolk, and his contact with them greatly enlarged his outlook. He succeeded in starting the theological school, but it proved short-lived owing to financial difficulties. All was infused with deep spirituality and a love of the principles of the Anglican Church.

In contrast, the new diocese of Truro, so remote, so poor and so full of dissent, would seem to be offering little. Benson was consecrated as bishop on 25 April 1877, and immersed himself in preparations for his reception and enthronement in Truro, on 1 May 1877. The morning of this

9

momentous day, so long awaited, was brilliant, sunny and calm. The rector and choir of St Mary's waited at the west gate of the churchyard in High Cross. The civic dignitaries approached in procession and were met and bowed into their seats. There was a very full church, cluttered as it was with high pews and memorials as well as the new seats for the Bishop and attendants.

Benson was solemnly installed as the first bishop of the restored diocese by his brother bishop, Temple of Exeter. The legal formularies, the long sermon and the Communion which followed lasted three hours; then there were speeches of welcome in the Town Hall. It was a day full of promise and hope, of triumph, yet tinged with sadness that some like Arthur Tatham had not lived to see it.

Obviously the first task for the new bishop was to familiarise himself with the diocese. Truro itself had already become a centre of Church activity and in county affairs too it was 'a rising place'. The building in the previous century of the Assembly Rooms and the town houses of the wealthy mining lords and the founding in 1818 of the Royal Institution all gave an impression of sophistication and culture. But beyond Truro, the task was massive.

Even the new diocese was vast in extent, comprising the whole of Cornwall, three Devon parishes and the Isles of Scilly. Many of the clergy lived in great isolation; the wide moors, deep inlets and jagged coasts together with sparse railway communication made it necessary for the Bishop to be often away from home, staying in some remote parsonage, manorhouse or windswept farm. Much evidence of pastoral neglect, eccentricity and poverty was apparent. Benson's son Arthur, who wrote fully on his father's ministry, his control of the family and the experience of Church life in Cornwall, has some portraits of clerical oddities and failures as well as some shining examples.

Benson would have found that many in the north-east of the county were not at all in favour of the Truro See, since they were much nearer to Exeter in distance and convenience of travel. He also encountered Methodism in the various groups into which it had divided since Wesley's death; he recognised its strength, especially among the mining communities, and acknowledged that during the slumber of the Anglican Church spiritual values had been kept alive in the chapels. Many

The interior of the old St Mary's church. The central aisle shown here was demolished but the south aisle to the right was restored as part of the new cathedral

villages were in fact without places of Anglican worship, either because the ancient parish church had been positioned by our Celtic ancestors whilst the villages had grown up in medieval times in a part of the parish remote from the church, or because new communities had arisen around a mining enterprise. Places such as Chacewater, Pensilva or Gunnislake, far from a church, teemed with mining families and were furnished with several chapels competing for adherents.

Benson's policy was simple: he encouraged clergy and wealthy lay people to build mission churches in every substantial village which needed one. They were to be staffed by lay readers. Many of these chapels-at-ease remain, some still in use, some as at Pencoys and Port Isaac now parish churches, and many others converted to secular use or demolished.

The gradual stirring into life of the diocese only showed up the complete inadequacy of the old St Mary's as a cathedral.

What might have been: J.P. St Aubyn's 1879 scheme to enlarge St Mary's as a cathedral. This was unacceptable to Bishop Benson, who wanted a 'true cathedral'

Apart from its elaborately carved south aisle, the building was in bad order. It was cramped, especially as stalls for the canons had been introduced; dignity of worship was impaired by the impossibility of reverent movement.

At the very first meeting of the Truro Diocesan Conference, in October 1877, a committee was formed to plan for an adequate cathedral. Its chairman then and throughout the building of the cathedral was the Earl of Mount Edgcumbe, whose determination and generosity carried the committee through many a time of perplexity and frustration.

The question was of course widely discussed, in the press and on the street corner. There was a good deal of opposition and polemic. Should a new cathedral be built on a new and imposing site? In that case a new Act would be required. Should St Mary's be extended over the old churchyard to the west as had been earlier proposed? A local architect, St Aubyn, produced a scheme for this with a long nave and a massive west tower. Many thought that this would suffice for a rural diocese, at a time when the mining industry was in economic recession.

But Benson wanted a true cathedral in the traditional sense on the St Mary's site, and invited seven architects to submit

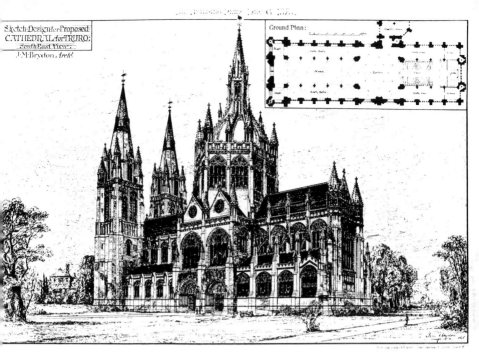

What might have been: J.M. Brydon's 1878 scheme for a new cathedral – prepared even though he was not one of the seven architects invited to compete. Brydon's most famous buildings are government offices in London's Parliament Square

designs for the cathedral or drawings of their recent churches. St Aubyn and R.P. Pullan submitted designs and five famous Victorian architects sent drawings – Bodley, Burges, John Oldrid Scott (son of Gilbert Scott who had just died) G.E. Street and J.L. Pearson. It seems likely that the brief included one central and two western towers, each with a spire, since all the surviving plans share these features. It may have been a sentimental idea of the Bishop's, reminiscent of the three towers (but without spires) of Lincoln.

Bodley received four votes from the committee, but Pearson was the winner with seven votes.

John Loughborough Pearson (1817-97) had established his reputation with several churches in London, of which St Augustine Kilburn is his masterpiece, and his great Gothic churches are probably the finest of their day in Europe. He had just designed the Deanery at Lincoln and a church at Devoran in Cornwall, and among many others was later to be responsible for the design of St Stephen, Bournemouth and Brisbane Cathedral in Australia.

13

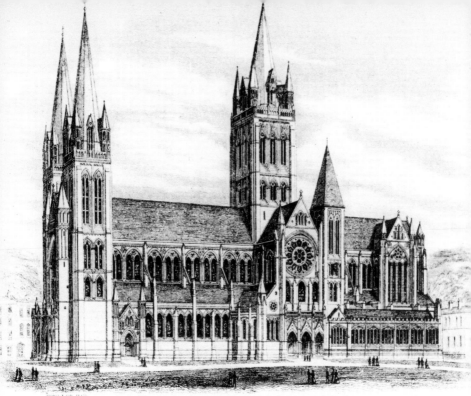

Truro Cathedral. South Front.

The architect's conception (all realised) of the finished cathedral, from a viewpoint impossible to see today due to the surrounding buildings. It shows the restored St Mary's aisle and the little parish church belfry to the right of the south transept, and the baptistry unusually placed to the left. The three towers and spires are Norman French in style rather than English, as is the unusual sexpartite vaulting of the nave which required external flying buttresses between *pairs* of windows. The square east end and secondary transepts are thoroughly Early English. Pearson's west front is inventive and original in having the nave project west of the flanking towers. The cathedral is a masterpiece of compression on the confined site, as it is only 275 ft long yet the central spire is 244 ft high

Pearson's attitude to church architecture was that it should be capable of arousing a sense of awe, of the mystery and majesty of divine worship. He loved the opening of new vistas as one moves around. There is always something more beyond, to see and explore.

Pearson's style is basically Early English, but he had travelled widely on the continent in his study of architecture and had

14

noted how the Breton and French cathedrals arose not from the green sward of the traditional close but among the shops and houses huddled at their foot. This was a necessity of the cramped site at Truro anyway but Pearson, sensitive to the affinity of Cornwall with Brittany, designed the cathedral accordingly. One can sense the almost Breton feeling of the cathedral today and its integration with the daily life of the community.

This continental impression gains strength from the attenuated appearance of the west towers, enhanced by long belfry openings, and within by the narrow and high proportions of the nave and choir. There is no structural division or screen dividing these parts of the building as is common in the ancient cathedrals of England. An open screen

A plan of 1892, showing the choir and transepts completed. The chapter house was not built as shown, nor any of the cloister garth. The plan shows some of Pearson's most unusual and inventive features: the nave aisle window screens and its sexpartite vaulting, with square central vaulting bays corresponding to two, rather than the usual one, window bays and alternate columns smaller in section; Pearson's favourite south chapel vistas and vaultings, here on either side of the south transept; together with the unusually placed baptistery and the additional narrow aisle to buttress the choir and form a link to the restored St Mary's aisle

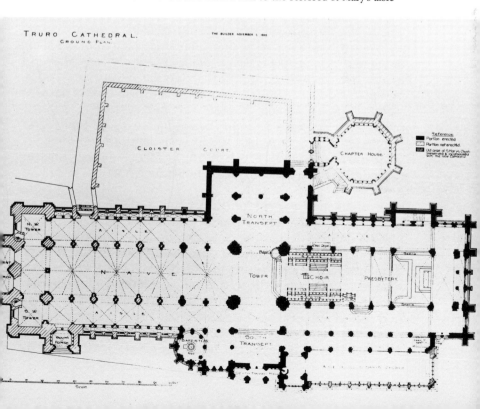

TRURO CATHEDRAL.
GROUND PLAN.

was proposed, and provision made for it in the great piers of the crossing, but objections were raised to it and it was never erected. There is therefore an uninterrupted vista of the whole length of the cathedral.

The way in which Pearson arranged the incorporation of the lower St Mary's aisle into the structure of the more lofty cathedral south choir aisle is noteworthy: he allowed for a second narrow south aisle whose tall pointed arches connecting the two act to stabilise the thrust of the main vaulting of the choir.

Pearson's work was enthusiastically supported by the committee and the Bishop, who was, however, suffering from a family tragedy the sorrow of which never left him. In the Christmas holiday of 1877 his eldest son Martin seemed unwell. He returned to his college at Winchester, but in February he died, it seems as the result of brain damage incurred in a fall some months previously. He was just seventeen.

3 Laying the foundations

Before the foundation stones could be laid, a great deal of preparatory work had to be done. As can be seen from the map, old St Mary's was on a restricted site except towards the west where the disused churchyard extended, with trees and a pump, towards the High Cross. On the north side was a narrow pathway on to which fronted the old rectory, a row of dilapidated cottages and the Bear Inn. All these had to be purchased and demolished to clear the land for building.

Meanwhile Pearson was working on the drawings for the cathedral and the question arose how much it would in fact be possible to save of old St Mary's. As a building it was undistinguished, except for the ornamented south aisle of the sixteenth century, and it was in bad condition. The Bishop himself did not desire 'the tinkering up of rotten stones'. But Pearson and the Committee considered it possible to restore the south aisle to a condition in which it could be included as a second south choir aisle, so retaining something of the parish church and preserving a continuity of civic history. This older part of the cathedral is now called St Mary's Aisle and is used as the parish church for the city centre. The rest of the old church was dilapidated and was not needed. St Mary's Street was so

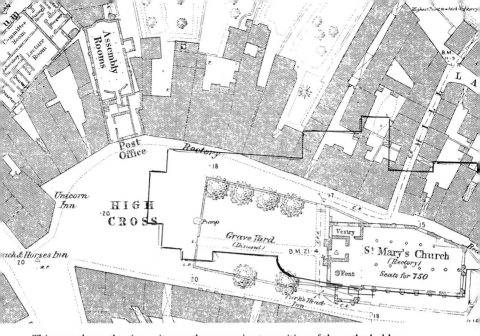

This map shows the site as it was; the approximate position of the cathedral has been sketched in and it can be seen how little space was available

narrow that the area of the prominent south porch was given to the corporation for road widening.

The west tower housed a clock made in 1770 by Richard Wills, the foremost clockmaker of the district, with two bells. Within, the old church contained some indifferent stained glass, which had replaced clear glass; this had been introduced in the 1760s, when the medieval windows had been thrown away. There was a sweet-toned organ by Byfield, given in 1750 when it had been one of the very few in Cornwall; it had originally been intended for one of the royal chapels, and is now housed in St Mary's Aisle. There was also a mahogany pulpit, and some good memorials to bygone Truronians including a tomb with two reclining figures commemorating the Roberts family: these prosperous merchants made a fortune from the tin trade, acquired a barony under James I and moved to the Bodmin area, where they built Lanhydrock House, changing their name to the more euphonious "Robartes". This memorial was apparently blackleaded during the eighteenth and early nineteenth centuries to preserve it!

Visitors will notice that the choir of the cathedral and the choir aisles are at a slight angle to the nave. This feature is not uncommon in medieval churches and fanciful and symbolic reasons have been suggested for it. Here it is entirely practical,

17

made necessary by the line of St Mary's Street and its narrowness, but it is also traditional.

The foundation ceremony was fixed for Thursday 20 May 1880. It was to be attended by the Prince and Princess of Wales (as Duke and Duchess of Cornwall) and was certainly one of the most memorable events in the history of Truro. The Prince (later Edward VII) and Princess travelled by rail to Grampound Road station, then were taken by carriage to Tregothnan, residence of Viscount Falmouth, where the royal party was to stay. At Probus they passed under a triumphal arch, the first of several erected for the occasion. Great crowds assembled and flags and bunting decorated the roads and streets to the cathedral site, as well as five more decorative arches. These had been designed by the Cornish architect Sylvanus Trevail, much of whose work survives in Board schools and other public buildings, and carried heraldic devices of prominent Cornish families as well as Masonic symbols. The actual ceremony was to be partly ecclesiastical and partly Masonic, since the Prince was Grand Master and other Masonic dignitaries attended with him. This inclusion of Masonic ceremonies was not to the liking of everyone, and adverse comment was made.

The procession passed under the arches at Boscawen Bridge; 280 members of the Metropolitan police had been brought to line the route, as well as various military detachments to provide security. The Mayor and Council waited at the Town Hall; speeches were made and replied to, then the Prince was taken to a house (Southleigh) in Lemon Street which had been transformed into a Masonic temple. Here he assumed Masonic regalia and with his attendants processed to the cathedral site. The officiating clergy and a crowd of others waited in St Mary's where prayers were said by the Bishop. Archbishop Tait was prevented from coming by illness. With Benson were the Bishops of Exeter and Madagascar, the latter a son of a former vicar of Kenwyn being on home leave.

There were two stones to be laid, one at what would be the north-east corner of the choir and another, the base of a pillar in the nave. The latter was of granite, and it was accepted that many years would pass before that part of the building could be attempted.

The Bishop of Truro was attended by his chaplain bearing the pastoral staff and also by two small servers in scarlet

The foundation stone ceremony on 20 May 1880: the Prince of Wales, later Edward VII, laying the memorial stone in the projected nave, before the west front of the old St Mary's; the main foundation stone had just been laid at the NE corner of the choir

cassock and surplice, with skull caps, following the body of clergy into the enclosure prepared next to the stone at the east end of the cathedral. There was a raised platform to which the Bishop, the Prince and other dignitaries ascended. After prayers, the foundation stone was laid by the Prince with Masonic symbols, the choirs sang a hymn accompanied by a band, and the Bishop gave his blessing. The western stone was then laid with similar ceremony; the visitor today can read the inscription on the granite pillar, but can also see the weathering caused by twenty-three years in the open air. After the final blessing, purses of money donated by individuals and organisations were placed on the stone, and totalled £1600 – a considerable amount at that time. Some four thousand people attended an open-air service the following Sunday.

The task of taking down old St Mary's began in October. The last services were occasions of some emotion, as the building had featured in many episodes of local history and many marriages and solemn obsequies had been performed in it.

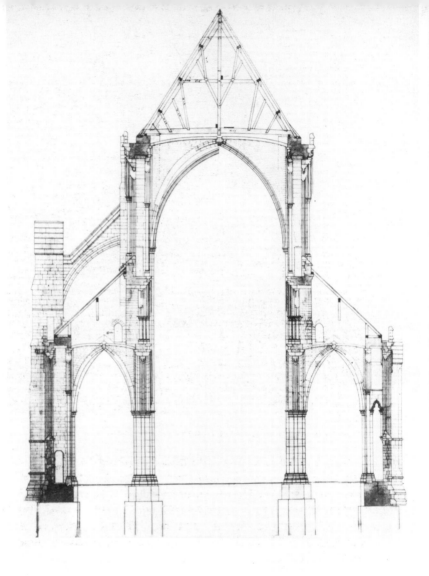

The architect's sectional drawing through the nave. The left hand side shows the
main points where the thrust of the sexpartite vaulting comes down to the
ground, with thicker columns and flying buttresses; the right hand side shows the
minor columns, slightly smaller and with no flying buttresses. These sections in
fact alternate from bay to bay. Above both the vaulted aisle walls there are cross
walls beneath the aisle roofs; and high above the nave there is a gap, as in
medieval cathedrals, with no structural connection between the stone vaulting
and the external steeply pitched timber roof

Construction starts in June 1882 with the choir

More than a hundred communicants attended the last communion, on Monday 11 October 1880 and the very last service was a marriage. The workmen entered the church and began demolition. The top few feet of the spire and the capstone were taken to Lis Escop and can be seen today near the Diocesan House, built in the grounds of what is now Copeland Court.

Financially it was impossible to build the whole of the cathedral in a continuous operation. The Committee and the Bishop decided it was important to start with the choir and its aisles, the great crossing and the two main transepts. The architect insisted that for structural reasons it was also necessary to build two bays of the nave and this caused some financial embarrassment, but gifts enough came in.

To cater for the services while the first part of the cathedral was being erected, a large wooden shed was erected on the north side of the choir area, costing £430. Into it went the fittings and ornaments from old St Mary's – font, organ, altar,

Timber scaffolding poles were used as in medieval times, lashed either with ropes or chains

pulpit and a large brass lectern given when the diocese was founded. This wooden 'cathedral' was bitterly cold in winter and stiflingly hot in summer! It remained in use for seven years, and saw many important events including the enthronement of the second bishop, Bishop Wilkinson, in 1883, after Benson became Archbishop of Canterbury. Ordinations, however, took place in the parish churches of Truro – St Paul's, Kenwyn, St John's and St George's.

One activity which originated in the wooden cathedral has become world-famous. For several years previously a late evening service had taken place on Christmas Eve in St Mary's, succeeding a still earlier practice where the choir had toured the town singing from house to house. The late evening service was partly designed as a counter-attraction to the public houses. For Christmas Eve 1880, Benson arranged in the wooden cathedral a service of nine short lessons, interspersed with carols, the readings being given by cathedral personnel from a chorister to the Bishop himself. This service of the Nine Lessons and Carols speedily became popular in many quarters, although its origin is largely forgotten and even claimed sometimes for other places. The wooden church and its place in Christmas observance is a touching remembrance.

When in time part of the cathedral building became available, the shed was sold and moved to Drump Road, Redruth, where it did duty for some years as 'The Cathedral Boot Works'; it survived until 1981 when it was destroyed by fire.

Thus was begun, in faith and high hopes, the cathedral church of the Blessed Virgin Mary in Truro, the first cathedral to have been erected on a new site since the sixteenth century. The brilliant weather on the inaugural day with the sky clear and unclouded and but a slight breeze to stir the bunting seemed to add to its blessings and to symbolise the peaceful and serene state of things towards the latter years of Queen Victoria's reign.

4 The Achievement

Visitors to the cathedral will notice the difference in level between St Mary's Aisle and the main part of the building. This arose from the lie of the land; under the choir there is a crypt, which accomodates the vestries. The crypt was necessarily the first part of the new building to be built.

The clerk of the works, responsible for the day to day supervision of the building, was James Bubb. He was a Londoner who had absorbed Pearson's vision and methods in previous works, a single man and a non-drinker, 37 years old when he came to Truro. His task was not an easy one: as well as responsibility for the preparation of the footings and foundations, he bore the brunt of some local anger at the demolition of the old cottages and was abused when he interrupted traffic in St Mary's Street to make theodolite observations. However his entire enthusiasm for the project carried him along. To Bubb and to Col. Cocks of Treverbyn was entrusted the choice of stone for the fabric. Pearson wanted Bath stone for the exterior but the majority opinion was that, although attractive and easily worked, it would not stand up to

The choir under construction in October 1882. To the right is the narrow buttressing aisle and beyond is St Mary's aisle, being restored

the Cornish winter weather without damage. Some 72 quarries were visited before Mabe granite was decided upon, with Bath stone details on the exterior, and for inside decoration a softer granite, Bath stone, polyphant, serpentine and other stones.

Before long a forest of scaffolding began to arise. At that time all scaffolding consisted of timber poles with rope lashings and much skill was needed to build it to the necessary heights.

From 3 December 1881, the workforce assembled each day for prayers and this practice continued throughout the erection of the cathedral, although later only weekly. When any important decision had to be made, a time of prayer always preceded it. When, for example, the sculptor Nathaniel Hitch was preparing to carve the central figure of the reredos, the crucified Christ, Bishop Wilkinson spent with him a time of intercession that the work would be worthy of its position and purpose.

The choir and eastern transepts full of scaffolding, May 1883

The choir workforce about 1883. There were never many more than 100 men employed, and only one serious accident occurred during the construction, when four people were seriously injured on a steam lift cage

Bubb was much put upon. He had to contend with the demands of his employers, the cathedral committee, with local difficulties and practical problems. Not all the employees were dedicated cathedral builders or men of prayer! Bubb sometimes worked nineteen hours in a day, and his health deteriorated; he succumbed to typhoid and died on 17 May

The rebuilding of St Mary's aisle in January 1883. It was Pearson's idea to retain the south aisle of the old parish church and link it through to his new cathedral

1882. He was succeeded as clerk by Robert Swain who remained in the post until the first part of the cathedral was consecrated in 1887. These two men carried an enormous responsibility for overseeing the detail of the workmanship, and should be remembered for it by everyone who enjoys the cathedral today.

Working on the west front, with a massive hoist and timber centering under the stone arches

All this mounting activity did not escape criticism by those who were aware of the cost. Benson when accused that 'You have drained Cornwall of money,' replied 'Yes, but not of zeal.' There was some point to the criticism as in the 1870s the county was experiencing almost total collapse of the mining industry, due to the discovery of cheaper ore elsewhere in the world, and there was massive emigration as a result, to many parts of the world where mining skills were in demand – South Africa, South America, Australia. 'Wherever there is a hole in the ground, you will find a Cornishman at the bottom of it,' it was said. Many villages saw almost half the male population leave, and this decline, despite a few temporary upturns and desperate attempts to diversify, lasted well into the twentieth century.

Some questioned whether it had been wise to embark upon so large and costly an enterprise, but Benson considered that the cathedral would give a focus and encouragement to the Church in Cornwall, not only to his own generation but to those which would follow. The building and its furnishing were supported by gifts from a multitude of people, great and small. Some few parishes, however, remained aloof.

Benson's leadership and character, his spiritual strength and deep knowledge, were nationally acknowledged when Archbishop Tait died, and the Queen's advisors suggested his name as Tait's successor. This choice greatly pleased her, and Benson was enthroned at Canterbury in March 1883. The new Bishop of Truro was George Howard Wilkinson, who had been one of his chaplains some years previously; this appointment meant that diocesan policy and the cathedral plans continued with little change.

It was thought fit to commemorate Benson's pioneering work in the diocese and as instigator of the cathedral. The south transept was built specifically to perpetuate his name and the tracery of the great rose window above it was given by the master and scholars of Wellington College.

The baptistry similarly recalls the heroic labours of Henry Martin, a Truronian who ventured as a missionary to Persia after a brilliant academic career. He translated the scriptures into the Persian and Armenian languages, and after his death was accorded the honours of an archbishop by the Christian inhabitants.

The north transept and the clock tower of the parish aisle, which is covered in Cornish copper, were also completed at

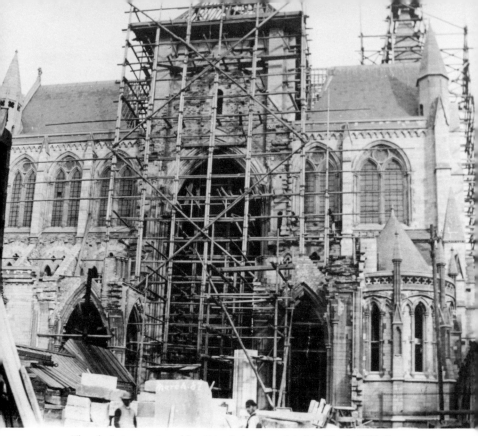

The choir, transepts and baptistry being completed in March 1887. Pearson insisted on having two nave bays to brace the crossing before this part of the church was capped and sealed off in 1887; the nave was not restarted until 1899

this time. The central tower, raised to the level of the lantern stage, was capped with a conical roof as a temporary measure. The temporary wall blocking off the western part of the crossing was saved from utter blankness by two galleries erected to give further accomodation at the consecration solemnities.

The shell of the first part of the cathedral now awaited furnishing. A great meeting of the women of Cornwall was organised, and there was a ready response in fund-raising activities; many of the basic fittings and ornaments remaining today result from the efforts of these good women. The bishop's throne is a memorial to Henry Phillpotts, subscribed for by clergy ordained by him. The four-manual organ, a masterpiece by Henry Willis, was installed in 1887.

The consecration of this part of the cathedral took place on 3 November 1887. Archbishop Benson returned to perform the ceremony, as usual full of enthusiasm for Truro. Once more the Prince of Wales came, and there was a feeling of universal holiday. About 2500 people crammed into all parts of the building: a body of workmen even found its way to the triforium. Nineteen bishops were present, besides the Archbishop and Bishop Wilkinson, when the building was blessed and the ornaments and furniture brought to their places for the Communion. Other services followed that day and after (the Deanery of Powder held its service on 5 November, to the amusement of many) and altogether some 10,000 people attended these services.

Now part of the cathedral was in use, and for the next nine years there was no further building. To have raised £70,000 for the endowment of the bishopric and nearly £120,000 for the cathedral was effort enough to satisfy Cornish churchmen for a generation. Parish and diocesan financial needs demanded attention. Nevertheless, although no specific appeals were made, bequests and gifts came slowly in for cathedral purposes.

It will be noticed that the south porch is elaborately ornamented, and forms the link between the more austere main building and the richer exterior of St Mary's aisle. This porch, named after Thomas Phillpotts who was vicar of Feock and nephew of the Bishop, has an interesting story. Thomas Phillpotts was a great admirer of a portrait of Lady Hamilton by Romney, owned by a friend. He used to ask to sit so as to admire it whenever he visited the house where it hung, and asked that if ever his friend should dispose of it he might have the first refusal. Years afterwards the friend wrote to say he did wish to dispose of it, and suggested a price of £50. Phillpotts replied that he could afford only £30, and this was accepted.

Some years later, the picture was exhibited at the Royal Academy while Phillpotts was on holiday in Rome. He received a telegram from a prominent dealer asking if he would part with it and if so to name a price. Phillpotts, never expecting to get it and only half seriously, asked £3000. Immediately the price was accepted. Phillpotts had some time before inserted a clause in his will that if the picture were to be sold, half the proceeds should go to the cathedral and therefore, although it happened in his lifetime, handed over £1500 for the erection of the porch which bears his name.

When in 1896 Benson died, an era seemed to have ended. There was a great desire to commemorate his Primacy, and a

Both these photographs show the completed choir and transepts from the north, one dated 1887, the other 1890, showing the double transepts (plus organ chamber) and the square Early English east end

tomb with recumbent effigy was proposed for Canterbury cathedral and the completion of the nave at Truro was also expected. A magnificent tomb was built at Canterbury but little money came the way of Cornwall. However, in faith the foundations were laid for the whole nave and the two western towers, under the direction of Frank Pearson, son of the original architect who had died in 1897, with Edward Price as clerk of the works. Before the nave was completed, the old Queen died in 1901; again there was a surge of desire to see the whole building finished as a memorial. A former resident of Redruth, Mr Hawke Dennis, offered to bear the whole cost of the 244 ft high central tower, to be known as the Victoria Tower, and it was started in autumn 1901.

Above: The masons' yard and the north aisle of the nave under construction. The flying buttresses every alternate window reflect the sexpartite nave vaulting inside

Opposite: The top of the hoist to bring materials up, with a little railway connecting to the bottom of the upper stage of the central tower

Following pages: The west end rises under a huge hoist. The cathedral construction techniques are still basically those used in medieval times. Notice the horse buses gathered at High Cross, and the cobbled street

It was not thought necessary to consecrate the completed nave, as it was mainly built over the old churchyard. Instead there was a Benediction service on 15 July 1903.

Once again the royal party attended, being met at the station not this time by carriages but by the High Sheriff of Cornwall's car, and once again they stayed at Tregothnan. But this time the Prince of Wales, Duke of Cornwall, was George, the former Prince being now King Edward VII. Twenty-seven bishops attended, besides the Archbishop and the third Bishop of Truro, John Gott. The Prince at the banquet which followed read a message from his father expressing 'my great satisfaction that you should finish the work which I commenced' – some twenty-three years previously. The great central tower was still not quite complete for this occasion. A screen was drawn across at the lantern stage. Some months later, at a formal ceremony, this was drawn aside to reveal the full inner height and beauty.

The completion of the western towers was again the occasion of special services in June 1910. They were made possible by a gift from Mrs Hawkins of Trewithen. A ring of ten bells was installed in the north-west tower; the architect had not really planned it for bells and some modifications were introduced to enable it to hold such a heavy and numerous ring. A proposal to hang a great bourdon bell in the south-west tower was abandoned, because of expense and the international tensions which were to lead to war.

It had been intended to connect the cathedral school premises, built on the north side, to the cathedral by a cloister, but in fact only one bay, given by the Masons of Cornwall in 1935, ever materialised. Other improvements and adornments have been added, however. The last piece of external statuary to be installed filled a blank vesica-shaped space over the north-west porch on the west front. It is the work of the late Guy Sanders, a local sculptor, and depicts the (very unwilling) submission of Kenstec, the last of the native bishops of the Celtic Cornish, to the Saxon Archbishop of Canterbury, Ceolnoth, in about AD 840.

The podium before the choir, a memorial to Archdeacon W H Prior, allows a free-standing altar to be used and ceremonies to be seen more clearly by the congregation. A general appeal in 1967 resulted in the gift of the Chapter House by the two grand-daughters of the Earl of Mount Edgcumbe, who had been such a faithful friend throughout the main building

The Prince of Wales, later to become George V, leaving High Cross with Queen Mary after the Benediction service on 15 July 1903

campaign. The Chapter House is designed as a crusader's pavilion and is intended to blend in with the cathedral style although in modern idiom. A cathedral shop in the north-west corner allows the visitor to purchase souvenirs, books and cards without disturbing the restful atmosphere of the main building.

This book has told the story of how Truro Cathedral came to be built as a result of the self-sacrificing gifts, devoted planning and skilful craftsmanship of a multitude of people in all walks of life. Their work witnesses today to a message which still needs to be heard, extending its welcome widely and ecumenically. Its aim, as that of Benson, Pearson and a host of helpers, is that Truro Cathedral should above all lift the heart and soul to the presence of God himself.

Statues on the Phillpotts Porch representing J.L. Pearson, the architect, holding the plan, and the Earl of Mount Edgcumbe, chairman of the building committee